SPACE LIBRARY

SPACE WALKING

GREGORY VOGT

FRANKLIN WATTS

NEW YORK LONDON TORONTO SYDNEY

Each new generation of humankind has had the challenge of a frontier. The frontier for today's children is outer space; it beckons with unlimited experiences. It is the frontier of my children, and I dedicate this book to them.

Kirsten, Allison and Catherine Vogt

First published in the USA
by Franklin Watts Inc.
387 Park Ave. South
New York, N.Y. 10016

First published in 1987 by
Franklin Watts
12a Golden Square
London WIR 4BA

First published in Australia
by Franklin Watts
Australia
14 Mars Road
Lane Cove, NSW 2066

US ISBN: 531-10142-8
UK ISBN: 0 86313 480 7
Library of Congress
Catalog Card No: 86-13273

Designed by Michael Cooper

Photo credits: All photographs courtesy of NASA, with the following exceptions: page 6 (both), National Air and Space Museum; page 8 (right) and page 10, Tass from Sovfoto; page 19 (left), Hamilton Standard, Division of United Technologies.

CONTENTS

TRANQUILLITY BASE, MOON

"I'm at the foot of the ladder. . . . That's one small step for a man, one giant leap for mankind." Those words were spoken by Neil Armstrong on July 20, 1969, as he became the first human to set foot on the Moon. It happened at 10:39 p.m. Eastern Daylight Time. Thirty-two minutes later Armstrong's partner Buzz Aldrin followed him to the surface of the Moon.

Nearly everyone at the time marveled at the fact that humans were able to travel 386,400 km (240,000 mi) from Earth to visit the Moon. The Saturn V rocket that carried them there was 111 meters (363 feet) tall, and its first stage burned 2.1 million kg (4.6 million lb) of rocket fuel in just two and a half minutes. By the time the astronauts left Earth orbit and headed for the Moon, they were traveling at a rate of 40,000 km/h (25,000 mph)!

The technology that made the trip to the Moon possible was certainly wonderful, but another bit of technology from the Moon flights, just as impressive, is often taken for granted. Armstrong and Aldrin were able to leave their lander and walk on the Moon's surface. People just accepted walking on the Moon as a matter of course.

Mankind's first Moon landing mission, Apollo 11, blasts off from the Kennedy Space Center on July 16, 1969.

(Left) Moonwalker Buzz Aldrin begins his climb down the ladder of the lunar lander at Tranquillity Base. (Right) Buzz Aldrin stands in a shallow lunar crater. Neil Armstrong is seen reflected in Aldrin's visor.

Why was walking on the Moon so remarkable? To answer that question we must know something about the environment of the Moon. It has no atmosphere, and therefore the astronauts had to carry all the oxygen they would need to last for several hours. Without air, there is no pressure on the Moon. Pressure is important because when it is taken away from living things, body fluids, especially blood and the water in the cells, begin to boil. The skin expands like an inflating balloon, and blood vessels to the brain are blocked by gas bubbles. It is like what happens when the top of a soda pop bottle is opened. In a short time, an unprotected astronaut would die a painful death.

Another unpleasant part of life on the Moon is that there is no air to protect astronauts from sunlight. The side of the astronaut facing the Sun is blasted with unfiltered sunlight, and the temperature quickly rises to more than 121°C (250°F)—considerably hotter than boiling point. The temperature on the side of the astronaut facing away from the Sun drops to minus 129°C (minus 200°F).

When we put it all together, an unprotected human on the Moon or anywhere else in space would be in great trouble. The human would suffocate, boil inside, and freeze and bake on the outside. Obviously, space walking is not something that humans are adapted for. Yet, twelve humans have walked on the Moon, and many more have space walked outside their orbiting spacecraft. They lived and worked in the forbidding environment of space and were comfortable. This was because of a special suit of clothes called a *space suit*.

How does a space suit protect its wearer? What is it made of and how does it work? What is it like to go space walking? How were space suits invented? What do space walking astronauts do?

EARLY SPACE SUITS

Now that astronauts from many nations fly into space on a regular basis, space walking strikes us as routine. But the high-tech appearance of space suits today wasn't something that just popped into the minds of engineers and scientists. Space suit development began almost thirty years before 1961, the year cosmonaut Yuri Gagarin became the first human to fly into space. It all began with a race to set an air-speed record.

One of these fast-flying people was American aviator Wiley Post. Post wanted to win the 1934 London-to-Melbourne race. His flying experience taught him that the higher he flew, the faster he could go. But he knew that flying high in the atmosphere meant that he would need some protection. The air was too thin up there to breathe, and he would need pressure for his body.

In June 1934, the B.F. Goodrich Company created a pressurized suit for Post. The suit was made of parachute fabric coated inside with rubber. His boots and sleeves had tight laces, and his head was covered with an aluminum helmet with a small glass window in the center. The window was small because Post was blind in one eye.

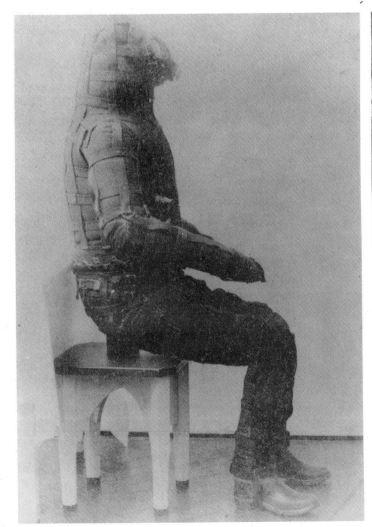

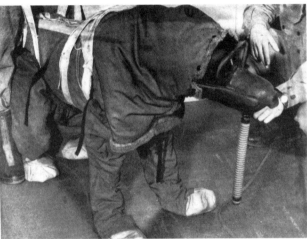

(Left) A German pressure suit of the 1930s. (Above) In the late 1950s dogs were suited up in order to study the effects of outer space conditions.

6

During a test, the suit blew open at the waist. Goodrich built a new suit and Post got stuck putting it on because he had gained some weight. It had to be cut to get him out of it. Suit number 3 was ready in time for the race but Post lost because the plane developed engine trouble.

Much was learned about pressure suit design in these early years. Research workers in Germany, France, Italy and the USSR were all interested in high flight and began constructing suits. They discovered that suits became rigid and uncomfortable when inflated. They were heavy and stiff. Some tried suits made of metal. Help was sought from companies that specialized in making armor, diving suits, tires, galoshes, and even girdles and corsets.

Over the years, many strange and wonderful suits were developed. Some looked like "bug-eyed monsters," and others looked like torture chambers. Along the way, pressurized aircraft cabins were developed, and then suits had only to serve as a pressure backup if the cabin pressure failed. This meant that the suits would not be pressurized except in the event of an emergency.

By the time of the first manned spaceflights in 1961 the best pressure suit designs consisted of two or more fabric layers. Joints and bearings (metal rings that permitted circular movements) were built in at points where the wearer needed to bend and turn.

(Left) Wiley Post waits patiently while the high-altitude pressure suit he is wearing is given a pressure check. (Below) Six years before it was needed, an early version of the Apollo space suit and portable life-support system was tested.

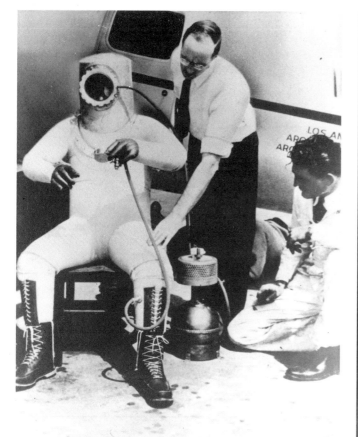

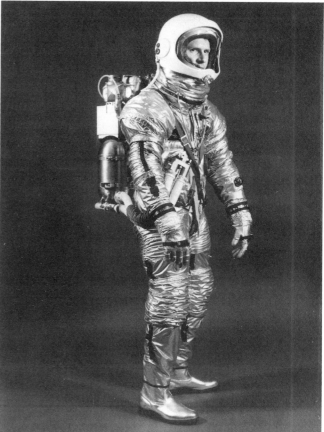

THE FIRST REAL SPACE SUITS

On April 12, 1961, Soviet cosmonaut Yuri Gagarin became the first human to travel into space. He orbited the Earth once in his Vostok space capsule before returning to the ground. Less than a month later, American astronaut Alan Shepard followed in a Mercury capsule. His flight, however, lasted only fifteen minutes.

In the span of less than one month the first two humans had entered the deadly environment of outer space and lived to tell about it. Both survived because their space capsules shielded them from all dangers. But what would have happened if their capsules had leaked? The answer was to place the person inside a second layer of protection: a space suit.

The suit worn by Gagarin had three main layers. The innermost layer was made up of insulating material. On top of that was a layer for holding air pressure against Gagarin's body. The outer layer was made of tough fabric to protect the second layer from punctures. A helmet with a double glass visor sealed the top of the suit, and gloves were worn on his hands.

Shepard's suit was simpler than Gagarin's. It consisted of an inner layer of rubber-coated fabric to hold air inside and a layer of aluminized nylon fabric on top. The nylon would not stretch and this meant that air inside the suit would push on Shepard instead.

Soviet cosmonaut Yuri Gagarin waits for liftoff in his Vostok space capsule.

A space suit with orange outer cover and helmet of the kind worn by Yuri Gagarin is displayed on a model.

To make it easier to move when the suit was inflated, metal rings were sewn in at the elbow and knees. Even with these rings, it was still difficult to move in the suit because bending squeezed the pressure layer in one place causing the overall pressure inside the suit to increase. Fortunately, for Shepard, the suit was worn "soft" without any pressure inside. It would pressurize only in an emergency.

(Left) Alan Shepard wears his space suit in a centrifuge test in which he will be spun around a large room in a simulation of the forces he will experience in flight. (Above) Shepard gets dressed for his suborbital flight.

The world's first astronaut team, pictured in 1959. The seven Mercury astronauts pose in their space suits. Front row (left to right) Walter Schirra, Jr., Donald Slayton, John Glenn and Scott Carpenter. Back row (left to right) Alan Shepard, Virgil Grissom and Gordon Cooper.

SPACE WALKING

Four years after Gagarin's historic flight into space, another Russian, Aleksei Leonov, became the first human to "walk" in space. Actually, no walking was involved. There was nothing to walk upon, but that is what everyone called his achievement.

In Earth orbit, spacecraft and humans are weightless. That means that if you were to step on a scale your weight would be zero. This is an interesting and exciting condition that few people ever get to experience. If you have ever ridden over a bump in a country road and felt your stomach go upward, you only got a hint of what weightlessness is all about. Another word for weightlessness is *freefall*. Imagine being in an elevator and the cables snap. You and the elevator car hurtle downward. Although you are in great danger, you would experience the feeling of floating because you and the car are falling together.

The falling elevator car is like an orbiting space capsule. The capsule is blasted into a high-speed path that travels parallel to the Earth's surface. Once in orbit, the rocket engines are turned off and the capsule coasts. The capsule is actually falling, but because of its speed the shape of the capsule's falling path is a great circle with the Earth in its center. It simply misses the Earth. The astronaut inside is falling at the same rate and therefore seems to float.

Cosmonaut Leonov was able to float freely outside his Voskhod-2 capsule on March 18, 1965. He began his space walk, or extravehicular activity (EVA), by opening the capsule hatch and pulling himself out into space. He remained attached to the capsule by a tether line. This prevented him from accidentally drifting away. Unlike Gagarin's suit, his suit had its own oxygen supply in a backpack unit. For twelve minutes, Leonov walked in space as far as 5 m (16 ft) away from the Voskhod.

After the flight, Leonov reported that his space walk went well. He did, however, have trouble reentering the capsule when he and a camera momentarily got stuck in the hatch.

The first space walker, Aleksei Leonov, floats outside his space capsule.

American space walker Ed White drifts outside his Gemini space capsule. The gold cord in front is his tether line to the capsule.

Ten weeks later on June 3, 1965, astronaut Ed White became the first American to go for EVA on the Gemini 4 mission. White's space walk lasted for twenty minutes. Like Leonov, White had a tether line, but his line also carried oxygen from the Gemini capsule and water to keep his suit cool in the searing heat of the Sun. During White's short space walk, he tested a device called the *hand-held maneuvering unit* that fired jets of gas to propel him around.

Ed White propels himself in space with the maneuvering unit held in his left hand. By aiming the unit in the direction he wanted to go, he could move as he wished.

WALKING ON THE MOON

So far, only twelve people have done it. During six Apollo missions twelve astronauts walked on the surface of the Moon. Prior to that time, astronauts had left their spacecraft just to see if they could do it and return safely. Those walks taught space suit designers how to build better space suits, what kinds of tools could be used and how to train space walkers.

The experience paid off. Neil Armstrong, the first to step on the Moon, cautiously took his time climbing down the ladder. Years before, scientists had suspected the Moon would be covered with a deep layer of dust that might act like quicksand. Armstrong saw that the top layer of dusty soil was not very thick because the lander footpads had sunk in only a few centimeters.

Practically the first thing Armstrong did after stepping off the lander was to collect a few samples of the soil and rocks and stuff them in his pockets. If something went wrong, requiring a hasty exit, he would not return emptyhanded.

Apollo 12 astronauts (left to right) Alan Bean, Richard Gordon and Charles Conrad are dressed in their space suits during a spacecraft checkout before their flight.

Soon his partner, Buzz Aldrin, joined him on the surface, and the two set up experiments and collected more samples. As they did their work, they bounded from foot to foot in what was later called a "kangaroo lope." The Moon's gravity is one-sixth that of Earth's, making it easy to hop from place to place.

Apollo space suits were a big development from the Gemini suits. The astronauts had to be able to move around freely and couldn't afford to be tied to the lander by an oxygen hose and tether line. The Moon suits needed their own life-support system. This was carried in a backpack unit called the portable life-support system, or PLSS (pronounced pliss). The PLSS contained oxygen for breathing and suit pressurization as well as cooling water and a radio transmitter.

With each Apollo landing, astronauts collected more samples, set up automatic science experiments and explored further from the landing site. With the Apollo 15, 16 and 17 missions, astronauts had a special treat. No more long walks for them. They had a snazzy Moon buggy to ride in. The buggy, called the lunar roving vehicle, or LRV, didn't look like much until it was unfolded. Each of its four wheels was powered by small electric motors. A couple of antennas and a television camera were mounted to the front and the astronauts sat in webbed seats that had storage bins for Moon rocks beneath.

In the low lunar gravity, the LRV's top speed of 14 km/h (8.7 mph) produced a wild bounding ride and its wheels kicked up large sprays of Moon dust. With LRVs the astronauts could explore more of the Moon's surface than they could on foot.

The Apollo flights to the Moon were tremendously successful not only because the astronauts reached the Moon, but also because they could walk on its surface and do scientific research. The six Moon-walking crews brought back a total of 382 kg (843 lb) of Moon rock and soil.

(Left) Apollo 15 astronaut James Irwin stands next to his lunar roving vehicle after one of several rides. The 3 by 2 m (10 by 6 ft) vehicle produced the V-shaped track in the foreground. The lunar lander *Falcon* stands behind Irwin. (Above) During the Apollo 16 mission, astronaut John Young leaps above the Moon as he salutes the U.S. flag. On Earth, Young and his suit and life-support system weighed about 160 kg (360 lb). On the Moon, however, they weighed only about 27 kg (60 lb).

REPAIRING A SPACE STATION

The launch on May 14, 1973 began just like the other nine Saturn V launches. However, there was one major difference. No one was on board. The rocket's third stage and the Apollo capsule had been replaced with the Skylab space station.

All seemed to be going well, but an hour after the launch, with Skylab in a 433-km- (269 mi) high orbit, mission controllers were still waiting for an automatic radio confirmation that Skylab's two large solar panels had opened. They soon learned that a meteoroid and heat shield had come off on the way to space. This broke the ties holding two large solar panels, causing one to be ripped off and the other to jam. The station was overheating and not receiving all the electricity it needed.

What could be done? The remaining panel had to be opened and the shield area covered. Eleven days later the first station crew took up residence on Skylab. The day after that, they suited up and opened an airlock located in the center of the missing shield area. They poked through long metal rods attached to an orange heat-reflecting cloth. It spread open like a four-spoke umbrella covering the damaged area. The inside temperature gradually dropped from 52°C (125°F) to a comfortable 24°C (75°F).

Getting enough electricity was still a problem, and that meant that the big solar panel had to be opened. Mission controllers weren't too happy about having the crew go outside the station, where there were pieces of sharp metal that could snag or cut a space suit. Furthermore, the area where the space walk would take place was never designed with space walking in mind. There were no built-in handholds. Yet a plan was devised that might work.

Skylab was NASA's first orbital space station. Three crews conducted scientific research on board for periods of twenty-eight, fifty-nine and eighty-four days. Skylab fell back to Earth in 1979.

Astronaut Jack Lousma of the second Skylab crew moves around the outside of the station to place a second heat shield over the one erected by the first crew to cover the missing meteor shield area. Hoses from his life-support system connect into the suit in the chest area.

Astronauts Conrad and Kerwin spent four hours outside in a difficult and daring repair effort. They first assembled a long pole with a bolt cutter at one end which could be worked by pulling a cord that stretched to the other end. After a little while, Kerwin got the cutters in position and Conrad held them there to keep them from slipping. While the two space walkers were getting ready, their spacecraft slipped in and out of darkness as it orbited Earth. Just at sunrise over the Indian Ocean, Kerwin pulled the cutter cord. The team effort worked and the panel popped open and locked into place.

Owen Garriott of the second Skylab crew "climbs" around the station's telescope mount after setting up a particle collection experiment. The large white package on his right leg is an emergency oxygen supply.

SHUTTLE SPACE WALKERS

The last Saturn rocket launch took place in 1975 when American astronauts met Russian cosmonauts during the Apollo-Soyuz space linkup. Following that, no other manned rocket took off from the United States for six years. During the six-year downtime, a new space vehicle was being constructed. This was the Space Shuttle and it was going to be unlike anything that had flown in space before. On April 12, 1981, the Space Shuttle *Columbia* blasted off. Instead of a cone-shaped capsule, the astronauts rode in style inside an airplane-shaped spaceship. It was launched like a rocket, operated as an orbiting spacecraft and returned to Earth as a glider so that it could be used again. By the time of the Shuttle's sixth flight, a new space suit had been designed.

Space suits used for the Gemini, Apollo and Skylab flights did the job they were intended to, but each suit was custom made. That meant that only the person the suit was built for could wear it. If that person got sick before a mission and had to be replaced by someone else, that suit could not be used. Furthermore, each astronaut needed three suits: one to be worn in space, another for training and a third to be used as a backup if the flight suit malfunctioned before the mission.

The Shuttle space suit's life-support systems are operated by the astronaut through controls mounted on a panel on the chest.

Shuttle space suits are tested for the first time on the Shuttle's sixth flight. Astronaut Story Musgrave (left) and Donald Peterson (right) float over the Shuttle's payload bay.

Making these custom space suits was quite an ordeal for each astronaut. Seventy different measurements had to be taken to insure a proper fit. In addition, astronauts get taller in space. A typical astronaut will grow up to 5 cm (2 in) taller in space. It's not true growth. What really happens is that on Earth, gravity causes body weight to press against the rubbery disks that separate the back-bones. In space astronauts float and pressure is off the back. The disks expand, pushing the bones apart. This produces extra height that is lost again back on Earth. Even though only temporary, the height gain must be allowed for when fitting space suits.

Just like the Space Shuttle itself, Shuttle space suits are reusable. An "off the rack" suit is tailored to fit. Suit parts (tops, bottoms, arms, etc.) are made in different sizes. When a suit is being prepared for an astronaut, the right-sized parts are selected to make the proper fit.

Story Musgrave works his way to the rear of the payload bay by sliding along a traverse wire.

DRESSING FOR SPACE

Shuttle space suits are called EMUs, which is the shortened name for Extravehicular Mobility Units. EMUs are much easier to put on and are more comfortable than earlier space suits. They have nineteen main parts, but most are already connected together so that the astronauts have fewer jobs to do when putting them on.

When it is nearing the time for a space walk, two Shuttle astronauts put on special helmets and begin breathing oxygen. This cleans out nitrogen gas from the bloodstream. Suit pressure is about one-third the normal (sea level) pressure of the Shuttle cabin. Any nitrogen gas in the blood would form bubbles, causing painful swelling in the knees, elbows and other joints.

Next each crew member puts on a urine-collection device. A tube, connected to a pouch, is used by male crew members. Female crew members wear a many-layered pair of shorts and use them like diapers. Then comes the liquid cooling and vent garment (LCVG). The LCVG is a suit of stretch fabric that is laced with tubes. Small tubes carry cooling water because space suits can become very hot inside. Large tubes circulate air through the suit to carry away moisture from perspiration.

Next come small but important tasks. A harness with electrical connections is put on around the chest. Antifog compound is rubbed inside the helmet. A food bar and a water pouch are inserted inside the suit chest for snacks and drinks while walking. Then the "Snoopy cap" radio headset is put on. When these jobs are done, the crew member pulls on the suit pants and then slides into the upper half of the suit.

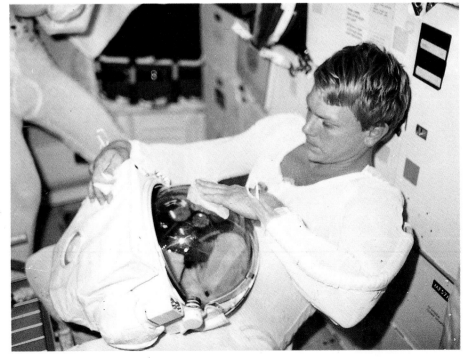

Mission specialist George Nelson wipes off his visor before donning the helmet. Nelson and James van Hoften are about to go into space to fix Solar Max (see page 26).

Under the upper portion of the suit there is a hard inner shell under the cloth layers. This shell provides a firm mounting point for the backpack life support system and front control box.

The helmet is a clear plastic dome much like an upside-down fishbowl. This is covered with a visor assembly that has a large dark sunshield and visors that can slide over the face when working in bright sunlight. When all is assembled, pressure checks are carried out on the suits to find out if there are any leaks. If everything is all right, the airlock door to the outside is opened and the space walk begins.

As they pull themselves through into the payload bay the two space walkers clip short tether lines to rings on the payload bay walls. This protects them from sudden movements that might bounce them out into the payload bay out of reach of any walls to grab on to. No matter what the job, the portable life-support systems on their backs can handle any demands. They can keep the astronaut cool even when doing hard work. There is enough oxygen for seven hours outside. All the time, the system cleans the air inside the suit of carbon dioxide and perspiration produced by the crew member. If something goes wrong, there is even an emergency oxygen supply which will last long enough to return back into the airlock and the safety of the orbiter.

Following the space walk, the two astronauts remove their suits and attach the upper portions to the wall inside the airlock. A hose and cable device from the orbiter is connected, and the suit's oxygen tanks are refilled, batteries are recharged and more water is added to the cooling system. The Shuttle space suits are now ready for space walks the next day.

(Left) astronaut Anna Fisher tries on her space suit. (Above) astronaut Story Musgrave practices putting on his suit during a zero-gravity training program.

FREE-FLYING SPACE WALKERS

In February 1984 American astronaut Bruce McCandless became the first free-flying space walker. Except for walking around on the Moon's surface, which isn't flying, all space walkers had been attached to their spacecraft by oxygen hoses or tether lines. These lines kept them from drifting away. Drifting off is easy. Then comes the problem of getting back. Since there is nothing out there to push on, you keep on drifting until the spacecraft comes to get you back. McCandless, however, had a new flying machine, called the MMU, or manned maneuvering unit, to get around with.

The MMU is a backpack unit that slips over the portable life-support systems that space walkers wear on their backs. When the user works the two hand controls, compressed nitrogen gas is released through small nozzles. This produces an action-reaction force that moves them through space. It works rather like a balloon when the air escapes through the opening, causing the balloon to fly away.

Though based on a simple idea, work on the manned maneuvering unit had begun more than twenty years before. Remember the twenty-minute space walk of Ed White on Gemini 4 in 1965? He tested a hand-held maneuvering gun that pushed him around with jets of oxygen. During the test, White remained attached to his capsule by a tether and oxygen line.

(Left) Astronaut Gerald Carr tests the astronaut maneuvering research vehicle inside Skylab in 1973. His hand-held maneuvering unit is similar to the one Ed White used in his space walk many years before. (Below) Bruce McCandless maneuvers near the Space Shuttle with his MMU. The small black dots near his knees are two of the unit's twenty-four nozzles. A camera is attached to the MMU above his right shoulder.

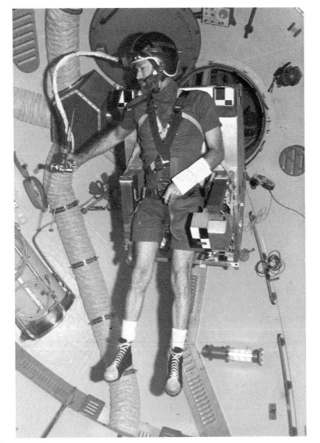

With his MMU, Bruce McCandless becomes an independent spaceship.

The next time a maneuvering unit was tested in space was inside the Skylab space station in 1973. The astronaut maneuvering research vehicle (AMRV), as it was called, was designed to be worn on the back. It had an open frame which held a tank of nitrogen gas. When two hand controls were worked, several of the fourteen nozzles spaced around the pack released the nitrogen, pushing the astronaut around. The AMRV unit offered much more control than White's unit but it was never used out in space.

The MMU worn by McCandless also used nitrogen for propulsion. In all, there were twenty-four nozzles arranged in eight three-nozzle clusters, one on each corner of the MMU. McCandless could move up or down, forwards or backwards, and from side to side. Furthermore, he could also do somersaults and cartwheels.

The gas supply on the MMU is enough for about a six-hour mission, depending upon how often the astronaut works the controls. When moving from one place to another, the unit can accelerate, or increase its speed, by about 1 cm (⅓ in) every second. That means the astronaut and the MMU can move 1 centimeter in the first second, 2 in the second, and 3 in the third.

As the test proceeded, McCandless flew 46 m (150 ft) away from the orbiter, stopped, returned and flew out again to more than twice the earlier distance. He later used a special latching mechanism to catch a target as practice for future rescue missions of disabled satellites.

After twenty years of development, astronauts were finally able to fly freely in space. In future flights, starting just two months later, the importance of the MMU would become very clear.

COSMONAUT SPACE SUITS

While the American astronauts were busy walking on the moon and designing a new Space Shuttle space suit, Russian cosmonauts were concentrating on manned space station research. They flew many space station missions and routinely began to surpass the 84-day spaceflight record of the last Skylab crew. Some cosmonauts have now spent more than one year in orbit above Earth on the Salyut 7 space station.

Cosmonauts have donned space suits and left their stations to do scientific and technological experiments, to perform repairs and make changes to their station, and to practice assembly and installation tasks in preparation for building larger space stations and spacecraft.

Like Shuttle astronauts, cosmonauts also have improved their space suits. Cosmonaut space suits are semirigid in design. That means that some parts of the suit are rigid and inflexible and others are soft and stretchy. The upper part of the suit has a hard shell that allows the life-support system to be mounted firmly to the back. Air and cooling water hoses are connected *inside* the suit so they won't get tangled or hooked on things during a space walk. This also enables them to mount a pressure control and monitoring panel and an emergency oxygen supply lever on the front.

(Left) Cosmonauts enter their space suits through the back door. A fellow crew member closes the door and checks the seal. Life-support systems are mounted in the door. (Below) A cosmonaut prepares for a space walk outside his space station.

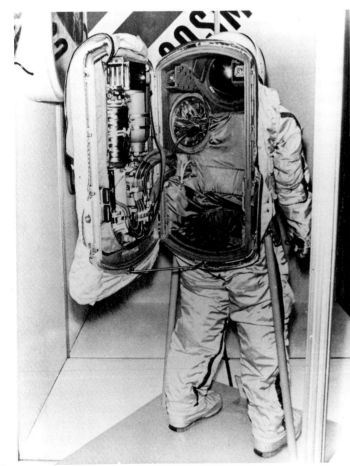

The suit arms and legs are soft. They can be adjusted in length while in space to fit the different cosmonauts who go on space walks. The one thing that is not adjustable is the gloves. Each cosmonaut has his or her own special gloves to wear on Salyut 7. Over a two-year period, four different cosmonaut crews living on Salyut 7 used the same suits on ten space walks.

Getting ready for a space walk aboard Salyut 7 is similar to going for a walk outside the Shuttle. Cosmonauts breathe pure oxygen before putting on their suits. However, because the pressure inside the suit is kept a third higher than Shuttle suits, their prebreathe period lasts only half an hour. They put on cooling suits that look like strange long underwear with tubes. Chilled water circulates through the tubes to keep the cosmonaut from overheating during the space walk. Next they put on their communications caps with earphones and microphones. After the oxygen prebreathe period is over, it is time to get into the rest of the suit.

After the cosmonaut has climbed in, another crew member seals the door. Except for putting on the gloves, the cosmonaut is now completely enclosed. The helmet is already mounted to the hard inner shell. If needed, a sun visor can be slid down over the clear "fishbowl" front.

While space walking outside the Salyut 7 space station, a cosmonaut photographs himself in the reflection of another cosmonaut's helmet visor.

TRAINING FOR WALKING

What is space walk training like? Often ground training is dull and involves classroom study and "pounding" the technical manuals to learn everything about the equipment. Cosmonaut space walkers learn how to fly the spacecraft so that if anything happens to the pilot they can take over. Shuttle space walkers, on the other hand, are trained to concentrate on the suit and on space walking tasks.

If a suit malfunctions it may be possible to repair it and get on with the walk. Future space walkers visit special laboratories to see every part of the suit and how it is assembled. They learn about the controls and how to monitor suit systems.

After becoming suit experts, it is time for the space walkers to try out what they have learned. The best places to learn about weightlessness without going into space are in airplanes and under water. The airplane is a large passenger jet with most of the seats taken out and replaced with padding along the walls, ceiling and floor. Astronaut trainees ride in the padded area while the plane climbs high above the Earth. At a designated moment, the pilot puts the plane into a steep dive, producing a condition of weightlessness. Everyone on board begins to float.

Weightlessness lasts for thirty seconds before the pilot pulls out of the dive and climbs again for the next dive. Just before pullout, everyone is warned to grab on to something or else their bodies slam against the floor. During each dive, the trainees try out different tasks, such as putting on space suit parts and getting used to moving things around.

Even though space walkers seem to "float," the job isn't easy. Preflight training is very important. Astronaut Bob Crippen wears a practice space suit on a training ride aboard the "Vomit Comet," a weightless training aircraft.

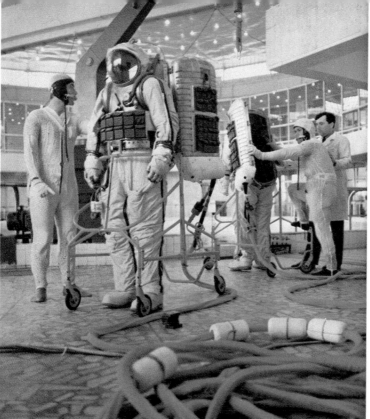

Cosmonauts prepare for underwater space walk training. The suits are weighted with lead to keep them from floating to the surface.

A calmer form of training takes place under water. This time space suits become diving suits. Heavy lead weights are hung around the chest and legs to keep the astronaut from floating to the surface. The idea here is to produce neutral buoyancy so that the astronaut neither floats nor sinks but appears weightless.

Underwater training has several advantages over training in aircraft. Underwater training can last for hours. Large replicas of the equipment used in space are submerged for practice. The one disadvantage of underwater training is that water is so dense that the astronaut can swim through it. This doesn't happen in space.

While safety divers watch, a cosmonaut moves around a space station model during underwater weightless training.

GETTING ON WITH THE WORK

In 1980 a satellite known as Solar Max was launched to study the Sun during a peak period of sunspot activity. After a while, the satellite's attitude control system began to malfunction and the satellite started a slow tumble, making it impossible for some of its instruments to aim at the sun.

Space walking astronauts George "Pinky" Nelson and James van Hoften were trained with one big goal in mind: to fix Solar Max. After the Shuttle was steered into a close orbit with Solar Max, Nelson put on his MMU and flew out to the satellite to stop it from tumbling. A special clamping mechanism was attached to the MMU to catch hold of the satellite. When stopped, the Shuttle could maneuver over to the satellite and bring it into its payload bay for repairs.

Before Nelson could clamp on, he first had to match the tumble of Solar Max with his thrusters. The satellite's attitude-control system fought against his efforts and continued to tumble. Though the capture attempt was unsuccessful, the MMU did exactly what it was supposed to do. A new plan was needed.

Back on board the Shuttle, meanwhile, satellite controllers on the ground succeeded in slowing the satellite so that the Shuttle's mechanical arm was able to capture the satellite and bring it inside the bay. Nelson and van Hoften again got into their space suits and went out into the bay with a repair kit. Van Hoften had to remove two dozen screws, detach panels, cut open insulation and rewire eleven connectors that held up to seventy-eight wires each. The operation was successful and the satellite was returned to orbit.

(Left) George Nelson tries to stop the slow tumble of the Solar Max satellite by using his MMU thrusters. (Below) Bruce McCandless practices using a tool that might be used on future satellite repair missions.

Astronauts Joe Allen and Dale Gardner move the large but weightless stranded communications satellite into a berth for its return to Earth.

A few months later Kathy Sullivan, together with David Leestma, practiced inflight refueling of a satellite's rocket-control system. This meant that in the future satellites could be refueled in space while they continued to do work.

The next actual space rescue took place one month later. Two communications satellites had run into problems when both of their booster rockets failed to fire properly, and they ended up in very low orbits. Astronauts Joe Allen and Dale Gardner were assigned to retrieve them from orbit.

Following the retrieval of the two communications satellites with the MMU, Allen and Gardner pretend to offer them for sale.

THINGS TO COME

Some of the new ideas for space suits and EVA equipment are strange and will probably never be used. One area that concerns designers is the possibility of a spacecraft being disabled and stuck in orbit. In such a situation its crew would have to be transferred to another Shuttle. There isn't room to carry full space suits for each crew member, so a mini–space suit, called the personal rescue enclosure (PRE), has been suggested for protecting crew members during transfer.

NASA is presently spending much time planning for a new orbital space station for the mid-1990s. Each part of the station will be carried to space in the Shuttle payload bay. Once in orbit, the parts will be assembled piece by piece. When finished, astronauts and scientists from all over the world will move on board and begin their work. EVA will be an important part of the building of the station and its routine operation.

The present Shuttle space suit will work for space station operations, but a more efficient suit would be desirable. The new suit is called the zero prebreathe suit, or ZPS. By doubling the suit pressure to twice that of Shuttle suits, no oxygen prebreathing period is necessary. However, the increased pressure would make the suit very stiff in the joints for arms, legs and fingers. But already the arm and leg joint problem has been solved, and the designers are concentrating on the hands. Some sort of robot hand might possibly be used with this suit.

A stranded astronaut is ferried inside a proposed PRE. The PRE is a pressurized ball of space suit fabric. A small oxygen supply inflates the ball to a livable pressure. When all crew members are wearing space suits or are safely inside the PRE, the airlock hatch is opened.

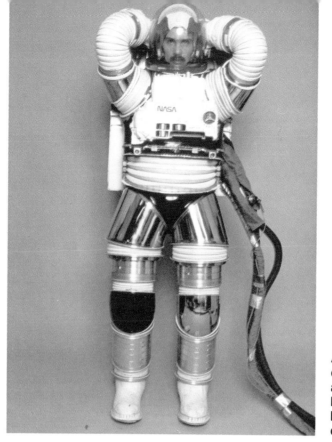

A space suit technician checks the ease of moving around with a version of the high-pressure zero pre-breathe suit for space station operations.

It is clear that there is much room for improvement in the space suits that astronauts wear and the tools that they use. Each new challenge requires new solutions. What will the challenges of the future be? The planet Earth is the only known place in our solar system where humans can walk around freely without any sort of protection. After space stations, we will certainly go back to the Moon to set up permanent stations and beyond there we will go to Mars, Venus, Mercury, the asteroids, and to other places billions of kilometers from Earth. And they will be places where space suits will most certainly be needed.

An artist's drawing of two astronauts working to align the pieces of a large space structure.

SPACE WALKING DATES

April 12, 1961 Yuri Gagarin became the first human to enter space and orbit the Earth.

May 5, 1961 Alan Shepard became the first American to enter space.

March 18, 1965 Aleksei Leonov made the first space walk.

June 3, 1965 Ed White made the first American space walk and was the first to use a propulsion unit to move around with in space.

July 20, 1969 Neil Armstrong became the first human to set foot on the Moon.

May 25, 1973 The crew of the first manned Skylab mission began a series of space walks to repair their crippled space station.

February 7, 1984 Bruce McCandless became the first free-flying space walker when he test-flew the manned maneuvering unit (MMU).

April 11, 1984 Space walkers George Nelson and James van Hoften made the first repair of a satellite (Solar Max) in space.

November 12, 1984 Joe Allen and Dale Gardner retrieved the first satellite (PALAPA) in orbit and prepared it for return to Earth.

GLOSSARY

Airlock A small chamber with inner and outer doors that permit an astronaut or cosmonaut to leave a spacecraft cabin without affecting the cabin's air pressure.

Apollo Project name for the U.S. manned space missions to the Moon.

Astronaut American name for someone who flies in space.

Astronaut Maneuvering Research Vehicle (AMRV) Rocket backpack used for maneuvering tests aboard the Skylab spacecraft.

Cosmonaut Russian word for astronaut.

Extravehicular Activity (EVA) Activity taking place outside the cabin of a spacecraft in which the astronaut must wear a space suit. Also known as space walk.

Extravehicular Mobility Unit (EMU) Space suit with life-support system.

Gemini Project name for the U.S. Earth-orbital two-astronaut space missions.

Hand-Held Maneuvering Unit (HHMU) Small rocket gun used by Ed White during his space walk on June 3, 1965.

Liquid Cooling and Vent Garment (LCVG) Inner layer of a space suit fitted with cooling water and air tubes.

Lunar Module Apollo spacecraft that landed on the Moon. Also called lunar lander.

Lunar Rover Electric vehicle used by Apollo astronauts to drive around on the Moon.

Manned Maneuvering Unit (MMU) Rocket backpack used by astronauts to travel in space outside the Space Shuttle.

Mercury Project name for the first U.S. manned space missions.

Meteoroids Particles of rock that travel through space at high speeds.

Orbiter Plane-shaped spacecraft portion of the U.S. Space Shuttle.

Personal Rescue Enclosure (PRE) Experimental sphere designed to protect Space Shuttle crew during emergency transfer between spacecraft.

Portable Life-Support System (PLSS) Backpack holding oxygen, electric power, cooling water, radio and other items needed by an astronaut wearing a space suit.

Salyut Soviet space station.

Skylab U.S. space station launched in 1973.

Soyuz Current manned spacecraft used by the Soviet Union.

Space Shuttle Current manned spacecraft system used by the United States.

Space Suit Pressurized garment protecting an astronaut from the dangers of the outer-space environment. Also called EMU.

Space Walk Extravehicular activity (EVA) by astronauts wearing space suits.

Stinger Device used by astronauts to capture two mislaunched satellites. Looks like a large insect stinger.

Vacuum An absence of matter. The condition found in outer space where there is no atmosphere.

Voskhod Three-astronaut Soviet spacecraft.

Vostok One-astronaut Soviet spacecraft.

Zero Prebreathe Suit (ZPS) Experimental space suit with sufficiently high pressure that no prebreathing period is necessary before going out into space.

INDEX

PRINTED IN BELGIUM BY
proost
INTERNATIONAL BOOK PRODUCTION